Contents

India today

India occupies the huge triangle of land poking out of the continent of Asia into the Indian Ocean. It is bordered by six nations: Pakistan, China, Nepal, Bhutan, Bangladesh and Myanmar (previously Burma). Two of its neighbours, Pakistan and Bangladesh, used to be part of India until the country was divided in 1947. India is above the equator, which means it is in the Northern Hemisphere.

India has nearly 17 per cent of all the people in the world. Or, to put it another way, every sixth person in the world is an Indian. Hindi and Bengali, two of India's major languages, are the fifth and sixth most-spoken languages in the world. With India's population fast approaching 900 million, only China has more people.

India is a confusing country. Its scientists and computer experts are among the best, capable of producing the most modern technology and successfully rocketing satellites into space. So it would seem to be a modern, industrialized nation. Yet in no other country do so many people work on the land and live in extreme poverty. For these reasons, India is still considered to be a developing nation.

India has about 40 large cities, each of which is home to more than 500,000 people. However, the majority of Indian people live in the country where facilities, such as education and health care, are limited.

In the desert state of Rajasthan, camels are an important means of transport, used even for delivering the mail.

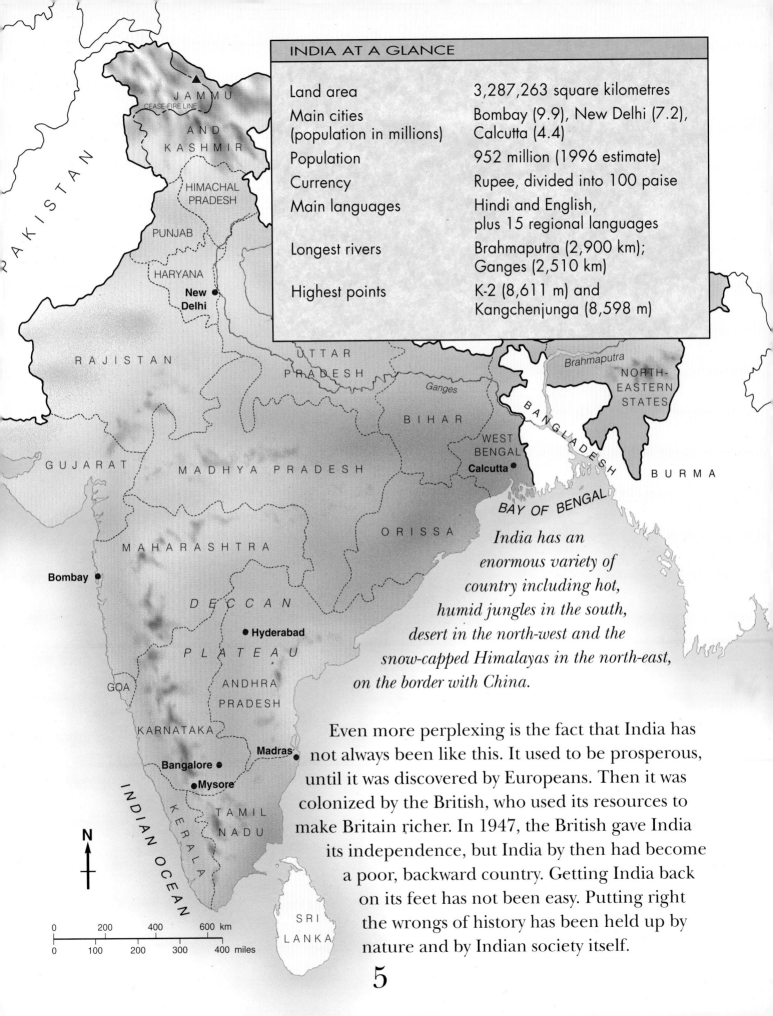

INDIA AT A GLANCE

Land area	3,287,263 square kilometres
Main cities (population in millions)	Bombay (9.9), New Delhi (7.2), Calcutta (4.4)
Population	952 million (1996 estimate)
Currency	Rupee, divided into 100 paise
Main languages	Hindi and English, plus 15 regional languages
Longest rivers	Brahmaputra (2,900 km); Ganges (2,510 km)
Highest points	K-2 (8,611 m) and Kangchenjunga (8,598 m)

PAKISTAN

JAMMU
AND
KASHMIR
CEASE-FIRE LINE

HIMACHAL
PRADESH

PUNJAB

HARYANA

New
Delhi

RAJISTAN

UTTAR
PRADESH

Ganges

BIHAR

Brahmaputra

NORTH-
EASTERN
STATES

BANGLADESH

WEST
BENGAL

Calcutta

BURMA

GUJARAT

MADHYA PRADESH

ORISSA

BAY OF BENGAL

MAHARASHTRA

Bombay

D E C C A N

Hyderabad

P L A T E A U

GOA

ANDHRA
PRADESH

KARNATAKA

Madras

Bangalore

Mysore

INDIAN OCEAN

KERALA

TAMIL
NADU

N

0   200   400   600 km
0   100   200   300   400 miles

SRI
LANKA

India has an enormous variety of country including hot, humid jungles in the south, desert in the north-west and the snow-capped Himalayas in the north-east, on the border with China.

Even more perplexing is the fact that India has not always been like this. It used to be prosperous, until it was discovered by Europeans. Then it was colonized by the British, who used its resources to make Britain richer. In 1947, the British gave India its independence, but India by then had become a poor, backward country. Getting India back on its feet has not been easy. Putting right the wrongs of history has been held up by nature and by Indian society itself.

5

The physical environment

India is the seventh-largest country in the world: roughly 3,200 km from top to toe and 2,700 km across at its widest point. People living at the southern tip are as far from New Delhi, the capital, as people in Athens, Greece, are from Londoners in England. Inevitably, communication is difficult within such a big country.

FARMLAND

Poor soils and a lack of water mean that only 55 per cent of India is fit for farming. Deforestation and overgrazing on much of the land have led to the erosion, by wind and rain, of topsoil from the northern highlands and the Deccan plateau. Fertilizers have to be used to encourage plant growth in the thin, stony soil that remains.

The best soil lies on the plains between the Himalayas and the Deccan, across which the River Ganges meanders to the Bay of Bengal. This soil is formed of a deep layer of alluvium, dropped over the centuries by the Ganges and its many tributaries when they flood. The alluvium is good for farming because it is rich in the nutrients that crops such as rice, wheat and vegetables need for good growth.

The most fertile land lies in the river valleys. Here, in the northern state of Ladakh, water from the River Indus is used to irrigate farming land.

THE IMPORTANCE OF THE MONSOON

No matter how good the soil, nothing will grow in it unless it is well watered. The farmers on the Ganges plains are fortunate because plenty of water is available from the river, via irrigation channels, and from under the ground. The rest of India's farmers have to rely on the monsoon for rain.

India has three seasons:

• Winter (lasting from October to February) is mostly warm and dry. Although temperatures plunge well below freezing-point in the Himalayas, they average 25 °C in the south.

• Spring (March to May) is hot and dry.

• Summer (June to September) is wet, and very hot, with temperatures soaring to 45 °C.

The rain is brought by the monsoon, a wind from the south-west. Blowing in from the equator, it picks up moisture over the Indian Ocean. The monsoon soaks the south first, usually around the end of May. Then, at a steady 20 km per hour, it moves across the whole country, reaching the north-west by the middle of July.

The monsoon is both a help and a hindrance. Some years it brings so much rain that there are destructive floods in much of India.

CLIMATE

New Delhi			Madras		
Month	Average temp (°C)	Average rainfall (mm)	Month	Average temp (°C)	Average rainfall (mm)
Jan	14	23	Jan	24	36
Feb	17	18	Feb	25	10
March	23	13	March	28	8
April	28	8	April	31	15
May	34	13	May	33	25
June	34	74	June	33	48
July	32	180	July	31	91
Aug	30	173	Aug	31	117
Sept	29	117	Sept	30	119
Oct	26	10	Oct	28	305
Nov	29	3	Nov	26	356
Dec	16	10	Dec	25	140

The monsoon is a mischievous wind, as it does both harm and good. Some years it arrives early and catches everyone unawares with a lot of rain. Floods can drown people and animals, wash away land and property, and generally cause chaos. In September 1980, heavy monsoon rains caused the River Ganges to burst its banks: 1,600 people died, 43,000 villages were flooded, and the city of Calcutta was knee-deep in water. In other years, the monsoon will arrive late and drop hardly any rain. Cattle die of thirst, farmers' fields dry up and people are threatened by food shortages. In between these extremes, there are years when the monsoon brings enough rain for good harvests.

Troublesome though it is, the monsoon is vital to millions of India's farmers. Although it blows for only a few months in the summer, the monsoon brings 70 per cent of all the rain falling on India every year. There is little rain during winter or spring, which means that some areas are dry for eight months of the year. Unless farmers can irrigate their fields during this time, they cannot grow any crops.

Length of Dry Season	Length of Wet Season
9 months or more dry	3 months or less wet
7-8 months dry	4-5 months wet
5-6 months dry	6-7 months wet
3-4 months dry	8-9 months wet
2 months or less dry	10 months or more wet
Growth interrupted by period of frost	

Although the amount of rainfall varies from region to region, it all falls during the monsoon season.

A water wheel, powered by cows, raises water from an irrigation ditch into a field.

Only 20 per cent of the farm land is irrigated, which means that 80 per cent of Indian farmers rely on the monsoon. They sow their seeds in the spring and harvest their crops, when the rains have stopped. They can grow little food until the following summer, when the monsoon will again provide water for their crops.

Earthquakes are another natural hindrance to India's progress. This man is clearing up after the 1993 earthquake in Maharashtra.

DESTRUCTIVE EARTHQUAKES

Life in India is also disrupted by earthquakes, which are common. On 30 September 1993, an earthquake shook 500 sq km of Maharashtra state. Lasting only seconds, it was powerful enough to kill 7,600 people and 2,100 cattle, to injure a further 217,300 people and completely destroy 18,800 houses. It will cost about £60 million to repair all the damage.

The effects of colonialism

Built in 1725, the Jantar Mantar observatory in New Delhi was used to revise the calendar and to check on ancient astronomical calculations.

Most people think that India benefited from the arrival of Europeans, that they, with their supposedly more advanced ways, generously modernized a backward nation to help the people living there. In fact, the reverse is nearer the truth, since there is much evidence to show that the Europeans did more harm than good to India. Instead of offering India a helping hand, the Europeans, particularly the British, held back India's progress – deliberately.

Europeans came to India in the 1500s to trade and to learn, for in many areas India was ahead of the rest of the world. European astronomers found that their Indian counterparts were using accurate tables for their calculations that had been compiled in 3100BC. They also discovered that Aryabhata, an astronomer working in AD500, knew that the earth was round and that a year lasted 365.3586 days. In 1790, Professor John Playfair of Edinburgh University, Scotland, concluded that astronomical observations were being made in India 'when all Europe was barbarous'.

Indian mathematicians provided the world with the zero, the decimal system, and a method of multiplication used in calculating machines before modern-day computers were invented. They were also working with many algebraic and geometrical formulae well before mathematicians in Europe.

In 325BC steel, called *wootz*, started to be made in India, long before it was made anywhere else. The production of *wootz* was complicated, one of the processes requiring temperatures of 1,200 °C. A sample of *wootz* was sent to London in the 1700s, where a scientist at the Royal Society said it was 'decidedly the best [steel] I have yet met with'. In 1842 British metallurgists praised the quality of Indian iron. Later, they were astounded to learn that it was made more efficiently and cheaply than in Britain, where new factories were meant to be the best in the world. A 7 m-tall *wootz* pillar in the Quitab Minar courtyard in Delhi does not have a speck of rust on it, despite having been in the open air since AD500. The reason it is rust-free continues to be a mystery.

Indian society, too, was well organized when the Europeans arrived. The farmers grew sufficient food throughout the year for everyone to be well fed. Their methods were a model of environmental friendliness. Doctors, using centuries-old remedies based on natural, medicinal herbs, kept sickness away. They knew about vaccination long before European doctors.

There was a good education system, with schools within reach of every village. Indeed, when the Europeans arrived, there were probably more literate people in India than in Europe. The arts and three major religions – Hinduism, Islam and Buddhism – flourished. India was far from being a backward country. If anything, the Europeans needed its help, rather than the other way round.

The Quitab Minar's iron pillar is about 1,600 years old. It continues to amaze people because it is free of rust, despite having been in the open air all the time.

THE EAST INDIA COMPANY

On 31 December 1600, the British government gave the East India Company permission to be the only British firm to trade with India. From then on, the company was in charge of selling British goods in India and Indian goods in Britain. It could keep everything it earned from this business. The company's owners were delighted: India was theirs and they could do whatever they liked with it. All they wanted to do with India was to make money from it – lots of money. For the best part of 300 years, the company saw India as a bottomless treasure chest which it could plunder to its heart's content.

The East India Company opened offices and factories in India, which it protected with its own army. Soon the soldiers were being used to conquer Indian rulers who were reluctant to trade with the company. Their lands were then taken over by the company. Eventually, the company was governing much of India. The British considered themselves superior to the Indians and showed them no respect, frequently ill-treating them. The company encouraged its staff to earn as much as possible, irrespective of the suffering they caused.

British Territory by 1805

Protected states

British Territory after 1856

KASHMIR

PUNJAB

RAJPUT LANDS

BENGAL

Calcutta

Bombay

Madras

The British did not directly control all of India, but their influence extended over the entire continent until 1947.

Indian people who defied the British rulers were swiftly put down. This drawing shows some being executed by hanging, and by being fired out of gun barrels.

12

> *'It is a country of inexhaustible riches and one which cannot fail to make its new masters the richest corporation in the world.'*
> – **Robert Clive, top official of the East India Company**

DESTRUCTION OF FARMLAND

The East India Company introduced a high land tax, forcing farmers to pay 50 per cent of their earnings. 'The idea,' as a company manager admitted, 'is to get as much as possible out of the *ryot* [peasant farmer] and when no more is to be got out of him, let him go to the Devil!' Many farmers could not pay the tax, so they sold their property to wealthy landowners, called *zemindars*. The *zemindars* allowed the farmers to remain on their land in return for paying them rent. Farmers who could not afford the rent were thrown off their land. If they were not replaced, the land went to waste. As a result, about 30 per cent of good farming land became useless, and food production fell.

The East India Company also reduced the amount of food grown by forcing farmers to plant cash crops – such as cotton, indigo, tea and jute – which were for selling, not for eating. Previously, enough food had been grown for some to be stored for the years when there was no rain. Now, there was no surplus food to put aside, so there were famines when the monsoon failed. The worst was in 1777, when 10 million people died in Bengal.

The company cut down many of India's forests to make ships and railway sleepers and so the land could be used for coffee and tea plantations. To ensure there would be enough timber for its needs, the company made laws to keep Indians out of the forests, and introduced a firewood tax. Consequently, cattle dung replaced wood as a cooking fuel. There was less dung to fertilize the soil, so much good farming soil lost its nutrients, and food production declined even further.

One of the worst famines in India's history was in the northern state of Bihar in 1770, where 30 per cent of the people died.

The skilled craftsmanship needed to build and to decorate this southern Indian temple shows how advanced India was when the British arrived.

EDUCATION

The East India Company's land reforms also affected the education system. Most schools had been self-financing. They had been given their own land, which they used to grow food for their staff and pupils, as well as a source of income to pay their running costs. The new land tax made this impossible, and many schools had to shut.

All the money raised by taxes went back to Britain. Before these taxes were introduced, this money would have stayed in India. India's raw materials, such as cotton, were also taken back to Britain and not used in India. The East India Company did not develop any industries in India, for fear that they would compete with the factories in Britain. Little was invested in India unless it was absolutely necessary. Much was spent on building railways, but only because they helped the British to get goods to and from the harbours.

In 1784, members of the British parliament, appalled by what had been going on in India, forced the government to shut the East India Company and to take over the running of India itself. By then, it was too late: India had been brought to its knees. Before the British arrived, India had been prosperous and self-sufficient. Now, the majority of its people were landless, ill fed, illiterate and poor. Farming land had been ruined and industries undeveloped.

'We did not conquer India for the benefit of the Indians. We conquered India as the outlet of goods of Great Britain.'
– Lord Brentford, speaking in 1931

14

INDEPENDENCE FROM BRITISH RULE

By the late 1800s, the seeds of dissatisfaction had been sown in India. An independence movement grew and gathered momentum in the 1920s, under the leadership of Mahatma Gandhi. His demands for the British to 'Quit India' and to give Indians *swaraj*, or self-rule, were finally answered in 1947, when India became an independent country.

The British may have left nearly fifty years ago, but India still has not recovered from their unjust, and often cruel, rule. It will take a long time for the scars of colonialism to heal.

By the 1930s, many Indians supported Gandhi in trying to force the British out of India. Here, police break up an anti-British demonstration in Calcutta.

'You have been taught that … British rule in India is beneficial. Nothing is more false! You cannot escape two facts: first, that under the British, India has become the world's poorest country; and second, that it is denied advantages and decencies to which any free country is entitled.'
– Mahatma Gandhi

MOHANDAS GANDHI (1869–1948)

Born in India, Gandhi studied in Britain before working as a lawyer in South Africa, where he helped to make the government repeal laws which were unjust to Indians. After returning to India, his peaceful protests against British rule encouraged rural people to follow his example and eventually force the British to leave. He was known as the Mahatma, or 'great soul', because his simple, honest lifestyle inspired Indians to rebel against their colonial rulers.

To millions of Indians, Mahatma Gandhi was just like them: he dressed and lived very simply. They followed him without question.

15

Measuring development

People often talk about the world's 'rich' and 'poor' countries. Poor countries are often referred to as 'developing', while rich ones have 'developed'.

There are many different ways of measuring how developed a country is. One way is to look at how much wealth a country produces, or its Gross National Product per person (or GNP per capita). This is the wealth created each year by its industries within its borders, plus the money earned from exports, divided by the country's population. The GNP per capita is the amount of money each person in a country would receive if all the wealth was shared equally. Obviously, the bigger a country's GNP, the larger each person's share would be. Rich countries would be able to give their people a lot of money, while poor countries would give theirs a small amount.

The wealth in any country is not shared equally. In India, few people are rich and many, such as this rickshaw puller, are poor.

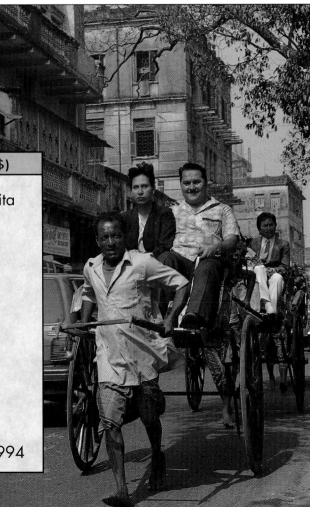

GROSS NATIONAL PRODUCT PER CAPITA ($)		
Rank		GNP per capita
1	Switzerland	36,080
6	USA	23,240
13	Canada	20,710
16	UK	17,790
17	Australia	17,260
22	New Zealand	12,300
105	China	470
115	India	310
123	Bangladesh	220
132	Mozambique	60

Source: *World Development Report*, World Bank, 1994

Poverty is obvious in much of India. Beggars in cities like Calcutta are often desperate for food.

Switzerland has the highest GNP per person, whereas India ranks 115th, out of 132 countries. In other words, Switzerland is the richest country in the world and India is the eighteenth poorest.

However, a single system such as GNP per capita can be misleading. No country in the world divides its wealth equally between all of its people. There are other ways of working out which are developed and which are developing countries.

According to some experts, for a country to be considered developed:

• there should be no poverty; its people should have the basic necessities of life: food, shelter, clothing, health care and education.

• there should be no unemployment; its people should have jobs to earn money for buying the things they need, and also for their self-respect – to feel that they are contributing something to society.

• there should be no inequality; everyone must be treated justly and fairly, regardless of their background, wealth or sex.

No country can completely wipe out poverty, unemployment and inequality. However, in a developed country these exist on a smaller scale than in a developing nation, where there are many poor people, high unemployment and great inequalities. Like any developing nation, India has its fair share of these three problems.

Even the children who go to school are poorly educated because their schools lack basic facilities such as classrooms, desks and textbooks.

POVERTY IN INDIA

India has some of the poorest people in the world, and not just a few million, but hundreds of millions of them. It has been estimated that 48 per cent of India's population (406 million people) are poor. (In Britain, 18 per cent of the population, or 10 million people, are poor.)

These people's poverty can be measured by the extent to which they are denied many of the basic necessities of daily life, such as clean drinking water, health care and education: the less someone has of these, the poorer he or she tends to be.

Providing them with more basic necessities would give them more opportunities to be better off, not only in terms of having more money, but in having a better life. Not having life's basic necessities is poverty.

For some people, it is difficult even to earn enough money to buy food.

WHO IS POOR IN INDIA?

In the Indian government's eyes, you are 'rich' or 'poor' according to whether you can afford to buy enough food for your minimum daily energy requirements. 'Poor' people cannot afford the minimum number of calories, while 'rich' people can. The government says that country people need to eat a minimum of 2,400 calories and city people 2,100 calories each day. (Country life is tougher, so rural people need more energy.)

18

INDICATORS OF POVERTY IN INDIA

- 63 per cent of Indian children under 5 years old are malnourished; Bangladesh is the only country in the world where the problem is worse.*
- An Indian woman can expect to live to 62, a man to 61; an American woman to 80 and a man to 73.*
- India has one doctor for 2,460 people; in the USA, there is one doctor for 420 people.*
- In India, there are 1,000 people per hospital bed; in Britain there are 200.**
- 14 per cent of India's population have access to sanitation and 73 per cent to safe water; in most Western countries, everyone has access to santitation and safe water.*
- 52 per cent of Indian adults cannot read and write; in European countries it is less than 5 per cent.*
- In India there is one teacher for every 60 primary school children; in Canada there is one teacher for 15 children.*

Source: * *World Development Report*, World Bank, 1994
**World Development Report*, 1990

It is difficult for the poor to break out of their poverty. The areas where they live have bad facilities, which means that they have very limited opportunities to better themselves. For example, because there are only a few schools people cannot get a proper education, which means that they cannot get a good job that pays well, so they get stuck where they are.

Unable to satisfy the basic needs of nearly half its population, India itself is a developing country. It cannot begin to think of itself as a developed nation until this level of poverty has been greatly reduced.

With no piped water in their homes, these men are forced to wash on the street.

Working in India

India does not have enough jobs for all its population. There is a high number of people who are either unemployed, or under-employed. The unemployed have no job whatsoever. Under-employed people have no regular, full-time job. Instead, they do odd jobs, perhaps working only for a few hours a week or for one or two days per week or month.

No one is very sure how many people are unemployed in India. However, after carrying out the population census in 1991, the government estimated it to be 36 million people, or 12.5 per cent of the total work-force.

DISTRIBUTION OF THE WORKFORCE		
	India	Britain
Agriculture	62%	2%
Manufacturing industries	11%	20%
Service industries	27%	78%
Source: *World Development Report*, World Bank, 1990		

Many Indians earn some money from part-time work because there are not enough jobs for everyone to work all the time.

There are probably the same number of under-employed people. In all, this means that about 72 million people, or 25 per cent of the workforce, are not receiving a proper wage. Assuming that these people have three dependants to support, then a total of 270 million or so persons' lives are affected by a lack of money.

As countries develop, it is usual for people to stop working on the land, and to find jobs in factories. In India, more people still work on the land than in industries because there are not enough factory jobs. The reasons for this are partly historical and partly connected with population growth.

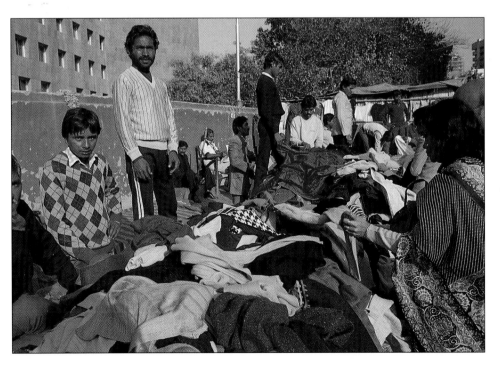

FEW FACTORIES

India has few factories, because its industrialization only started after Independence. The British had used India as a source of cheap, agricultural raw materials. Instead of turning India into a nation of factory workers, the British made sure it stayed a nation of farmers. The only factories built in India were for processing crops, ready for shipping them back to Britain. Jute and cotton mills, for example, were constructed to prepare the raw farm crops for the factories at home. Independence from Britain gave India the freedom to start industrializing.

In 1947, industries employed less than 10 per cent of the workforce. Today, they still employ only 11 per cent of the total number of workers.

Most of India's industries are located near the coast, to be close to transport by ship.

N

New Delhi

Calcutta

Bombay

Goa

Bangalore

Madras

○ Steel plant
▽ Oil and Gas
▲ Oil refineries
■ Major port
◆ Major iron ore mine
✶ Petrochemical plant
▽ Space centre
◇ Shipyard
□ Nuclear power station
△ Aircraft manufacture
+++ Railway

TOO MANY WORKERS

The other reason for India's high unemployment and under-employment is population growth. Although industries have been built quickly, the population has grown even faster. Every day, 70,000 babies are born in India – nearly one per second – and the population has been growing by 2.3 per cent per year, or over 19 million people. (In comparison, the population of Britain increases by 0.2 per cent per year.)

'I didn't want seven children; my husband did. He wanted to impress his friends. He also thought the children would make him rich, but they've only made us poorer. It's so expensive now to educate, feed and clothe them that I've told my eldest daughter to stop at two children, no matter what her husband says.'
– Tulika Kapoor, a mother from Delhi

In India, there are more small workshops, like this one in Calcutta, than factories.

THE IMPORTANCE OF AGRICULTURE

As there are few factories, city jobs are scarce. Most people who go in search of them are disappointed. They end up doing odd jobs and increasing the number of under-employed. The other alternative is to remain in the countryside to work on the land. Agriculture employs 62 per cent of all workers.

A minority make a good living from the land. They are people with large farms in good areas – mainly on the Ganges plain – where they can grow enough for their own needs, and still have a lot of surplus crops to sell for an income.

However, the majority of people in agriculture are either subsistence farmers or labourers, both of whom scratch a living from the land. The subsistence farmers can grow enough to feed themselves, but little or nothing is left over to sell. Many of them farm in areas where the soil is poor and where there is no irrigation during the dry season. They do not have the money to improve their land, and have to do the best they can with their limited resources.

A farmer's wife drying coriander seeds. She is fortunate in having enough land so that some crops can be sold for an income.

THE 'GREEN REVOLUTION' – SUCCESS OR FAILURE?

The Green Revolution is the name given to the changes in agriculture in the last twenty years. The most important one was the introduction of new types of wheat and rice, called high-yielding varieties (HYVs), which increased the size of harvests. However, HYVs required a lot of fertilizers, pesticides and regular watering. Rich farmers could afford to plant HYVs: they had the money to buy the fertilizers and the pesticides and improve their irrigation systems. Poor farmers had to borrow money, which increased their debts. Often, they have not been able to keep on buying the fertilizers and chemicals, so their HYV crops have failed. In much of India, the Green Revolution has only made rich farmers richer and poor farmers even poorer.

22

Winnowing the wheat harvest in Ladakh. The soil there is frozen for several months during the cold winters, so nothing can be grown in it and farmers have no work.

Rice, wheat and maize are the main Indian crops.

Agricultural labourers earn their money from working for farmers, perhaps by helping them to gather the harvest or to sow seeds. Most of their work is seasonal and dependent on the weather. If the monsoon fails or washes away the crops, they get no work. Most agricultural labourers are under-employed.

The 1991 census estimated that 6 per cent of all agricultural male workers were unemployed. However, when the numbers of under-employed were included, this rose to 23 per cent. In 1991, 191 million worked in agriculture, so about 44 million men did not earn full wages.

Even if they had been in full-time work they would have earned little. India's population boom has been most noticeable in the countryside, for this is where the majority of the people live. While the number of rural workers has increased, the amount of land, and therefore the number of jobs, has remained the same. As there are more people wanting work than there are jobs available, wages are low.

Rice

Forest

Highland pasture

Unproductive land

Arable wheat and maize

MONEY FROM FARMING

Each year the amount of money India earns from agriculture gets smaller. This shrinking sum has to be shared by more and more people, which means that farmers and agricultural labourers are worse off. In fact, recent studies show that they are earning the same as they did in the 1950s. The cost of living today is, of course, much higher.

This Delhi teenager has probably been working for ten years already, to boost his family's income.

For the majority of families, income is more important than education. Many children start working as soon as they can walk and talk.

CHILD LABOUR

The high numbers of unemployed and under-employed adults have caused an increase in the number of children who work since Independence. With their fathers earning little or nothing, the children are used to top up the family income. There are few job opportunities in the their villages, so the children are sent to the nearest town or city, where they do anything offered to them: from pavement shoe cleaning and being the errand boy in a hotel, to jobs in factories or workshops.

Once again, except from the fact that child labour is widespread, no one knows how many children work. However, it seems safe to assume that if an adult replaced every child worker, there would be little unemployment or under-employment in India, and millions would be better off.

'I never went to school so I cannot read or write. I've been working for as long as I can remember. I sell snacks to the people on the Maidan, the huge park in the centre of Calcutta.'
– Arun, aged 13

24

*'The employment of children triggers a cycle of illiteracy,
indebtedness, indignity and poverty. For every child employed, there
is an adult unemployed. Adult unemployment leads to poverty;
poverty leads to child labour; child labour results in lack of
education and stunted physical and mental growth which in turn
leads to unemployment in adulthood. Obviously this vicious circle is
the greatest threat to national progress – it is a national disaster.'*
**– Ksailash Satyarthi, South Asian Coalition on Child Servitude
(an organization which is trying to put a stop to child labour)**

Most employers 'buy' children from parents desperate for money. The employers look upon the children as their slaves, treating them badly, paying them little and making them work long hours in unhealthy conditions. Many children start working at a young age. For example, a recent study of the carpet industry found that 300,000 children were employed in it, 18 per cent (54,000) of whom were under ten years old.

*A silk-weaving workshop.
Most of the workers in this
industry are children, who
work in bad conditions
for little money.*

25

Street children of Bangalore

Bangalore is the capital of the southern state of Karnataka. It is one of the biggest cities in India, with a population of 3.3 million. Bangalore is the 'Silicon City' of India, full of booming computer and electronics businesses. Space satellites are also made there and launched nearby. These new industries have made Bangalore one of the richest cities in India. Despite this, over 40 per cent of its population lives in slums. Unable to make ends meet, many families have been forced to send their children out to work. Most of them end up on the streets. Here, they are joined by the children who have left home because of family problems brought on by the stresses of slum life and poverty.

There are 45,000 children living and working on Bangalore's streets. About 25,000 of them stay on the streets the whole time, both day and night. Some are orphans with no family to support them. Others have left home because they have been unhappy there. Some of these children keep in contact with their parents, others want nothing to do with them. The remaining 20,000 children work on the streets in the day and return home in the evening with what they have earned.

One of Bangalore's many homeless children keeps warm at night, before curling up to sleep somewhere on the street.

The children who have to go out to earn money work in dark, dusty conditions. They grow up with bad eyesight and breathing problems, which will stop them working. When they become adults, they may be forced to send their

Sorting used lottery tickets before taking them to a recycler, who will sell them to a paper mill.

The ages of the street children range from five or six to late teenagers. About 60 per cent of them are 'rag pickers', who rummage through rubbish for waste, such as paper, plastic or cardboard, for recyclers. In return, the recyclers pay them a few rupees per kilo or give them food and shelter.

Living on the streets brings the children into contact with the criminals of Bangalore. They often tempt the children into theft, prostitution or dealing in drugs. The children are constantly harassed by the police and they are sometimes kidnapped by 'slum agents', who force them to work as virtual slaves in factories or hotels.

> *'My parents live in Bangalore. They are drunkards. They used to hit me and shout at me every day. In the end I left home and went to live on the streets. That was six years ago.'*
> **– Padmanabham, aged 16**

children out to work. Poverty is the cause of child labour, which causes further poverty and more children being employed to support their families. It is a vicious circle in which millions of Indians are trapped.

Inequalities in society

Although India has become a wealthier country by industrializing, its wealth has not been shared equally between the cities and the countryside. Industries have developed around the cities and it is here that the wealth they have generated has been spent. The countryside has not benefited. For example, the number of country people who can read and write is half the number of people living in the cities. In the villages, nearly twice as many babies die before the first birthday as in the cities. In other words, there are more schools and better health care in the cities than in the countryside, and there are more poor people, and greater poverty, in the countryside.

'We work harder to make up for the money lost by sending two children to school, but it's worth it. My wife and I have suffered because we can neither read nor write. We don't want our children to have the same problems.'
– Jangaiah, farm labourer in Andhra Pradesh state

Only the richer city people can afford a scooter for transport.

India is a nation of country people: nearly 75 per cent of the population lives there, in 578,000 villages. The villagers' most important possession is land. It provides them with food, for eating or selling. Cows can be grazed on it to supply milk and dung, which is both a fertilizer and a fuel. Land can be used as security to obtain a loan.

In India, the land is owned unequally: a few people own a lot of it and millions none of it. In between these two groups are the millions of subsistence farmers who own small plots. The British were responsible for this inequality in land ownership. They encouraged the *zemindars* to seize the land of the peasant farmers who could not pay their land tax. The *zemindars* ended up with huge areas of land, which their families still own. Today, it has been estimated that 3 per cent of the population owns 40 per cent of the land. Since Independence, laws have been made to redistribute the land more fairly. However, the laws have not been obeyed and landless people have lacked the confidence to complain.

Most large landowners abuse their powerful positions in rural society. They rent land to landless people in return for a share of the harvests. Frequently, this is an unfair share which leaves the farmers with only just enough to survive on. Other landless people work as labourers for the large landowners, who pay them low wages.

A rich landowner in Gujarat state. Many people who own land have grown wealthy by treating other people unjustly.

29

People come to the large landowners – who are the richest people in the country – to borrow money. They will be lent it on condition that it is repaid at a high interest rate. Many borrowers fall behind with their repayments and sink further into debt. It is not unusual for the debt to grow so big that it cannot be repaid in the borrower's lifetime, so it is passed on to his children. Whole families can end up in 'bonded labour' to a money-lender, working solely for him until an inherited debt is paid off.

Country people can have a difficult life. If they have no land, they are in the power of greedy landowners. But even if they have their own land, they are still at the mercy of the monsoon. If the rains do not come, or flooding occurs, they may not have enough food. Often, the only way many people can survive is by borrowing from the money-lenders.

Country people try to improve their lives by having many children. In developed countries, large families are seen as a drain on income: the more children you have, the more it will cost you to feed, clothe and educate them. Indians take the opposite view: children can earn money to increase the family income. Many families now rely on their children for incomes. Children can also look after their parents in old age, something that is important in a country where pensions and old people's homes are rare. Because of the low quality of health care in villages, many children die young. In order to ensure that a few of them survive to adulthood, parents have many children.

Most country people think that large families are a help, not a hindrance. This potter's children can help him with his work so that he can earn more money.

TYPICAL MEALS EATEN BY COUNTRY PEOPLE	
Breakfast:	In the north, *paratha* (thick pancake); in the south *idli* (rice dumpling) and a spicy sauce.
Lunch:	Rice, *dhal* (lentil soup), and vegetables, or, in the south, *masala dosa* (stuffed pancake).
Dinner:	Rice, vegetables pulses and *chapatis* (thin pancakes).

Opportunities for entertainment, as well as work, are more plentiful in cities than in the countryside.

While this may help individual families to survive, it worsens the situation for country people as a whole. Already, there are not enough resources for the existing people, so more people will mean that everyone is worse off. For example, land is one of the most scarce resources. The more children in a family, the smaller their share of land on their father's death. The smaller the land, the more difficult it is to grow enough to eat. In the end, a rapidly expanding population threatens the availability of land. It is a country person's most important possession; life is miserable without it.

As India's cities have developed, millions of country people have left the land and moved to them in the hope of having a better, and easier, life there.

CITY LIFE

City life rarely lives up to the hopes of most rural migrants. Once the rural poor, they are now part of the urban poor. They remain on the lowest rung of the social ladder. Even so, few of them regret their decision to leave their villages, because they now have access to a wider range of facilities, from basic necessities to leisure activities, such as cinemas and parks. There are also more opportunities to earn an income, especially for landless people. Previously, their jobs had been seasonal and affected by the weather. In the city, the jobs are more regular, come rain or shine.

31

There are not enough factory jobs for the thousands of rural people who arrive in the cities every day. Most of the migrants end up doing a variety of odd jobs. The industrialization of India has created a wealthy middle class of city business people who require workers in their offices, factories and homes. Employees, too, are needed by the new industries, shops, restaurants and hotels opened to cater for the demands of this new class of people, many of whom have a lot of money to spend. Their incomes equal those of wealthy people in developed countries and they aspire to a similar lifestyle, with designer-label clothes, expensive cars, foreign holidays and all the latest household machines.

Educated and with good jobs, these two city women have lifestyles which country women can only dream about.

THE CASTE SYSTEM

Hindus are divided into four social groups, or castes:
- At the top are the Brahmins, from whom the priests are chosen.
- Next are the Kshatriyas, the soldiers and officials.
- Then come the Vaishyas, the business and crafts people.
- Finally, there are the Sudras, the farmers.

Separate from these castes – literally, 'out-castes' – are the Untouchables, the people with the dirtiest jobs. Today, they prefer to call themselves Dalits, which means 'the oppressed'. They comprise 16 per cent of the population.

Generally, people in the higher castes have the best opportunities in life. For example, 53 per cent of all government officials are Brahmins, even though Brahmins make up only 3 per cent of the population. In the countryside, the upper castes own most of the land, while the lower castes are more often landless.

In country villages, each caste often has its own neighbourhood – with the Dalits living separately – and people marry only within their own caste. In many villages, if a Dalit were to drink from a Brahmin's well, he or she would be stoned to death.

Fuelled by rural migration and the middle class's money, India's cities have exploded in size. Between 1971 and 1981, they grew by 45 per cent; Bangalore alone by 77 per cent. They have reached bursting-point. Public transport groans under the weight of double the number of passengers it was designed to carry; power stations cannot cope with the increased demand for electricity; nor can sewage pipes with the greater amount of waste.

Although they are affected by the problems, the wealthy urban middle class has the resources to cope with them. They have smart homes, cars, servants and generators for their air-conditioners. The urban poor have none of these, so they suffer the most. For example, there is a major shortage of housing in all the cities, which means that homes are very expensive. Unable to afford them, millions of poor people are forced to live on the streets, and in shacks in dirty slums, where diseases spread rapidly in the hot climate. In 1990 the Indian government estimated that 48,800,000 people lived in slums in India, the majority of them in the cities.

INDIAN CINEMA

India is the word's largest producer of films. Each year, it produces over three times as many movies as the USA.

A lack of housing means that many village people end up living in filthy city slums, like this one in Delhi.

'We thought that city life would be better. We've ended up in a shanty town on the banks of a stinking river full of garbage. We live in a hut made of bits of wood and plastic we've found. It leaks in the rain. There's no electricity and no water, and the children always seem to be sick.'
– Santosh Kumari, hotel porter in Delhi

The Indian government does not have the money to look after this deformed man, so he is forced to beg to survive.

SOCIAL INEQUALITIES

There are many divisions within Indian society which prevent people from improving their lives.

Caste is the biggest barrier to progress. It is very difficult for members of the lowest castes to get a good education and an important job. By law, a percentage of university places and government jobs has to be given to low-caste people. However, putting this into practice has not been easy. Caste is less of a problem in the cities, but in the country it is still a handicap.

Before Independence, Pakistan and Bangladesh were part of India. In 1947 it was decided that India would be a Hindu nation and that the areas where the Muslims lived would become separate Islamic countries. However, many Muslims continued to live in India. Although by law there is no religious discrimination, there is rivalry between the two religions, which often breaks out into violence, and Hindus tend to be given preference over Muslims.

India has traditionally been a male-dominated society. In the cities, there is now more equality between the sexes, but in the countryside the men still make all the important decisions.

RELIGIOUS GROUPS	
	Percentage of population
Hindus	82.6
Muslims	11.3
Christians	2.4
Sikhs	2.0
Buddhists	0.7
Jains	0.5
Others	0.5
Source: *India Book, 1994–95*, D M Silvera	

INEQUALITY BETWEEN THE SEXES

India is one of the few countries in the world where there are less women than men. Men are valued more than women because they have traditionally been the income earners, while women have stayed at home. As women usually do not earn money, they are expected to bring some wealth with them when they marry. This is the reasoning behind paying a dowry: that is, the bride's family present her future husband with jewellery, furniture, clothes and, if they are rich, a car or motorbike. Even though dowry payments have been banned by law, many families still expect to receive them.

Parents, whether they are rich or poor, consider daughters a burden because dowry payments usually land them in heavy debt. Often, poor families will not look after a daughter properly and so many girls die young. In the poorest regions of India, some families take more drastic action: they kill their daughters at birth. A booming business in the cities are clinics where a pregnant women can discover the sex of her foetus. If it is female, it will be aborted.

MRS INDIRA GANDHI

Indira Gandhi was the daughter of Jawaharlal Nehru, the first prime minister of Independent India. She also entered politics and became prime minister herself from 1966–77 and 1980–84. Although many of her policies were controversial, she was a strong leader who was devoted to national unity and to the reduction of poverty.

Despite the lowly status of many women, education, wealth and a tough personality all helped Indira Gandhi (bottom right) reach the top in politics.

'Girl killing is also traditional in parts of southern India, particularly in the poor Salem district of Tamil Nadu . . . 51 per cent of families in Salem killed baby girls within a week of their birth to avoid dowry, currently running at around 60,000 rupees – the equivalent of 50 months' wages for an unskilled worker.'
– The Times of India *magazine, 5 March 1994*

Development: improving people's lives

A European doctor helping at health clinic which receives money collected by charities abroad.

Non-governmental organizations (NGOs) are groups of people who have been helping India's poor since British times. The first NGOs were British missionaries and charity workers, who opened churches, schools, hospitals and orphanages. While the poor benefited from their 'good works' in their daily lives, these early NGOs could not halt the number of people who were becoming poor.

In the 1960s, the NGOs decided to adopt a different approach. They thought the solution lay in improving conditions by doing things like digging wells for irrigation and providing better health care. While this was an improvement on the earlier good works, the poor were rarely consulted about what they wanted and little was done to end the social problems which caused poverty. A well may have cured a water problem in a village, but it did nothing to stop a powerful landowner robbing the villagers of their land. The Indian people knew this was the real problem, but they had not been asked about it. A lot of money was wasted on unnecessary projects and the poor continued to grow in numbers.

Providing clean water often helps people to live more easily, but the underlying causes of poverty are often more difficult to solve.

Nowadays it is accepted that the best way to tackle poverty is to ask people about their problems and let them suggest the best ways of solving them. Only in this way can people be helped to help themselves, so that in the future they will not need any outside assistance to lead better lives. This approach also tackles many of the social reasons behind long-term poverty.

Most NGOs in India have concentrated on working in the countryside, where poverty is at its worst. Raising the level of literacy is now considered to be one of the most important ways to improve people's conditions. People without an education are open to all sorts of unjust treatment, which holds back their progress. Money-lenders, for example, can cheat them because they cannot read a loan agreement. Once people can read and write, they are more aware of their rights under the law, which gives them the confidence to challenge people who mistreat them.

As well, educated people are open to new ideas. When mothers attend literacy classes, their children's health also improves, because the teachers often discuss such matters as child care, diet and hygiene. Educated people can learn more easily how to take better care of their children. The chances of their children living to adulthood are much greater, thus reducing the need for such big families.

Village women being taught how to use sewing machines so that they can start their own clothes businesses.

'We are being trained to work sewing machines as part of a scheme to increase job opportunities for women. At the end of the course, I can take a sewing machine back to my village. There I will make clothes to sell, as well as train other women to help me.'
— **Dolma, from a mountain village in Ladakh**

Although it is certainly a bonus, education on its own cannot help landless people to earn a living. If, however, they are taught a skill – perhaps a craft such as weaving or carpentry – they may find regular, better-paid employment. Alternatively it may help to have money to start their own businesses.

NGOs can help with special loans, at low interest rates, so that a newly trained tailor, for example, can buy a sewing-machine without getting into expensive debt with the local money-lender. Farmers, too, can take advantage of these loans to purchase things that will improve their ability to grow food, such as high-yielding varieties of seeds, fertilizers and pesticides, or to dig wells or irrigation channels.

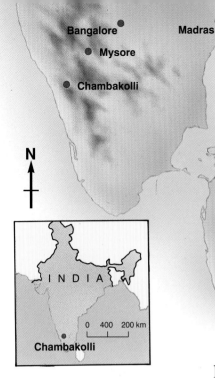

Chembakolli is located in the far south of India. The nearest town is 30 km away, down rough dirt roads. Mysore, the closest city is another 100 km distant.

DEVELOPMENT IN CHEMBAKOLLI

Chembakolli is a remote village among the forested hills in the southern state of Tamil Nadu. It is home to a community of Adivasis, people who are the descendants of the original inhabitants of India. The 51.5 million Adivasis are out-castes, like the Dalits, and live throughout central and southern India. They are mostly subsistence farmers. In Chembakolli they grow rice, onions, tomatoes, peppers and oranges for themselves, plus a little tea and coffee as cash crops.

Rejected by society, the Adivasis are illiterate, own little land and have very limited access to health and education. In the past, their communities have been badly organised, so they have been unable to prevent the government and rich landowners taking away large areas of their land and cutting down the forests. Now, their future is under threat.

Since 1987, an Indian NGO, ACCORD, has been helping the people of Chembakolli to overcome their problems and to fight for their rights. ACCORD has been encouraging the villagers to act together, telling them that they have more power as a group than as individuals. At their regular community meetings, or *sanghams*, the villagers were soon listing all their problems, deciding how urgent each was and taking the appropriate action.

'We know that any problem can be solved because we are a group, not just individuals. We are not afraid any more.'
– *Kelu, who regularly attends sanghams in Chembakolli*

A sangham in Chembakolli, where people work out how to solve problems that affect them all.

Before doctors visited Chembakolli regularly, people had to walk many miles if they needed medical help.

IMPROVING LIFE IN CHEMBAKOLLI

Money was an issue worrying many people, so ACCORD helped the villagers start a co-operative credit scheme, into which everyone pays two rupees a month. The money is loaned out, for example, to pay off debts to landlords and money-lenders, to buy seeds or to build a house. It is repaid at a very low rate of interest.

The credit scheme is also used to pay two doctors to visit the village regularly. They treat the sick, as well as giving advice on staying healthy. They vaccinate children against polio and measles and hold classes on baby care for pregnant mothers. As a result, fewer babies are dying in their first year and children are living longer. The doctors have also trained health workers in Chembakolli to look after and advise the villagers between their visits.

Buying tea seedlings with the village credit scheme has allowed some people to increase the amount of money they earn.

The villagers realized that tea would be a good cash crop, to earn extra money. However, they were short of money to buy the tea seedlings and confused about the ownership of suitable land. The village credit scheme provided the money for the seedlings and ACCORD assisted in sorting out the land-ownership matters.

'Tea used to be the big man's crop. We knew it would be good to grow but we never had enough money for the seeds. Now we have our own land and seeds we can plant in it.'
– Karunakan, who now grows tea on his land

ACCORD has also helped to open a school in Chembakolli. Previously, Adivasi children had gone to local government schools, which they did not enjoy. The children felt very inferior to their upper-caste class mates. The new school is run by villagers who have been trained as teachers by ACCORD. They understand that education is not just about reading, writing and arithmetic: it must make the Adivasi children proud of their culture and confident in their dealings with other Indians, whether Dalits or Brahmins. The teachers also emphasize the need to take care of the environment, for as it deteriorates so do the Adivasi's chances of a better life.

The Adivasi children find it easier to learn at their own school.

'When I was a child, I went to a government school. There was only one other Adivasi child there. We used to wear gold ear-rings, which the other children made fun of. They couldn't understand our language. The teacher told us not to speak it in school, but didn't tell us why. For twelve years I felt that everyone was superior to me.'
– Penchi, who sends his children to the new school

STREET CHILDREN

All of India's street children miss out on education. Living on the streets also affects their health, both physically and mentally. They do not grow as tall as other children because they have a poor diet, sometimes eating food from waste bins. Long after others have grown up, street children are still behaving like children half their age.

Working towards a brighter future

In Bangalore, several NGOs are helping street children to get a better start in life. Several NGOs have opened shelters which are home for some children, while others just visit them during the day. As well, they are helping the children by teaching them skills which will allow them to get jobs. Some shelters give the children food, health advice and classes in carpentry, screen printing, tailoring and electronics.

'On the streets my biggest problem was food; also the police used to arrest me and I had to pay them money to get away. Now I'm in [a] shelter and I wear decent clothes, eat and wash every day. My lessons are also helping me to start planning for the future. None of this would have happened a few years ago.'
– Bijl, aged 10

Bijl, on the left, now has hope for a better future since he began going to the shelter.

Outdoor pursuits also help to give the shelter's children the confidence to cope with challenging situations.

Children over 16 can go to another NGO after they have learnt a skill. The staff try to find them jobs with local firms, most of whom are usually reluctant to employ ex-street children. To make it easier for them to get employed, the teenagers are

'Local employers want responsible, reliable, honest workers – qualities they don't think street children have. My job is to convince them that they're wrong. You can find these qualities in our teenagers.'
— **Solomon Jayaprakash, who works in a shelter**

'I've been working as a garage mechanic for one year. It's a great job and I would like to open my own business one day. Without help, I'd still be a rag picker, and I never want to go back to that.'
— **Lokech, one of the shelters' success stories**

taught the skills they need to keep a full-time job. There is also an effort to build up their self-confidence with outdoor activities, such as rock-climbing, which encourage them to tackle difficult tasks.

India tomorrow

Many tourists visit India. The money they bring into the country is an important source of income.

Cut off by the high Himalayas, Ladakh has missed out on India's post-Independence prosperity.

There is no doubt that India made a great leap forward since Independence. In 1947 only 15 per cent of adults could read and write; few could expect to live beyond their late twenties; there were frequent food shortages; hardly any villages had electricity; and there was very little industry. Even so, despite the progress, today India has twice as many poor people as neighbouring China, which has a bigger population.

Mahatma Gandhi believed that poverty could be reduced if India concentrated on improving conditions in the countryside. As the countryside prospered, Gandhi said, it would push the rest of India forward: India would develop from the bottom up.

Jawaharlal Nehru, Independent India's first prime minister, believed the opposite: India should advance from the top down. Nehru gave priority to heavy' industries in the belief that they would pull India forward, with all Indians benefiting from the progress.

Will the wealth created by India's new industries 'trickle down' to these street sellers?

Today, the government continues to follow Nehru's line of thinking. It considers that the wealth created by the rich people at the top will trickle down to the poor below them. The government anticipates that the richer the middle class becomes, the more it will buy. Then, more factories will have to be built and more jobs will become available for the poor. If this happens, all India's people will be better off.

Even if this plan works, it will be many years before there are any noticeable benefits. Until then, India's poor will need to be supported so that they are in a better position to improve their own lives.

FOREIGN DEBT

To help pay for India's industrialization, the government has had to borrow money from the World Bank. This loan rises every year with a high rate of interest. In 1997, it was over $92 billion. Every year, India has to use 13 per cent of its earnings from exports to repay this debt. The further into debt India gets, the more difficult it is for it to help its own people.

Glossary

Alluvium Earth or sand left behind by flood or river waters.

Astronomy Study of the sun, moon, planets and stars in the sky.

Calorie A unit of energy produced by food.

Census An government count of all the people in a country.

Colonialism When a country is controlled by another country that is usually richer and more powerful. The controlled country becomes a colony.

Deforestation Cutting down large areas of forest.

Debt Owing money to another person or country.

Dependant Someone, such as a wife or child, who depends on another person to earn money.

Famine Not having enough food for anyone to eat.

Fertilizer Something added to the soil to make it better for growing crops.

Gross National Product (GNP) The money a country earns within its borders, plus money from exports.

Illiterate Being unable to read or write; signs of a poor education.

Independence When a colony becomes free from foreign rule.

Indigo A blue dye, for dying cloth such as cotton, obtained from a plant.

Interest rate The money that has to be repaid regularly to pay for money that has been borrowed.

Irrigation Adding water to land to grow crops when it would otherwise be too dry.

Jute A fibre obtained from the bark of a plant, used to make sacks and mats.

Life expectancy The number of years a person can expect to live.

Literacy Being able to read and write.

Loan Money that has been borrowed.

Malnourished Not having enough food to eat.

Migrant A person who has moved from home to live in another town or country.

Monsoon The name of the wind that brings the summer rain; the rainy season, too, is often referred to as 'the monsoon'.

Overgrazing Allowing animals on pasture to eat too much, so that the land becomes bare. This often leads to soil erosion.

Pesticides Chemicals used to kill insects, to stop them from eating and destroying crops.

Raw materials Materials in their natural state, such as coal, iron ore.

Recycling Turning rubbish and waste into something that can be re-used.

Sanitation Drains and pipes for removing waste.

Service industries Industries, such as tourism and banking, which do not make goods, but supply people with services they need.

Soil erosion The wearing away of the soil by wind or rain.

Subsistence Growing food or earning money that is just enough to live on.

Tourist Person from a different country who is on holiday.

Zemindars Large landowners, who became powerful under British rule.

Further information

Addresses and Websites

ActionAid, Hamlyn House, Archway,
London N19 5PG
Tel 0207 282 4101
Website: www.actionaid.org

Oxfam: 274 Banbury Road,
Oxford OX2 7DZ
Tel: 01865 56777
Website: www.oxfam.org.uk

Christian Aid: PO Box 100,
London SE1 7RT
Tel: 0207 604444

Development Education Association,
3rd Floor, Cowper Street,
London EC2A 4AP

Save the Children Fund
Mary Datchelor House,
17 Grove Lane, London SE5 8RD.
Tel: 0207 703 5400.

Unicef: 55-6 Lincoln's Inn Fields,
London WC2A 3NB
Tel: 0207 405 5592
Email: info@unicef.org.uk

Books to read

Asia (*Continents* series) by David Lambert
(Wayland, 1997)

A Flavour of India by Mike Hirst
(Wayland, 1999)

Chembakolli Photopack and slide set
looking at life in a village in southern
India. (ActionAid)

India (Country Fact Files series*)* by Anita
Ganeri (MacDonald Young Books, 1997)

India (*Country Insights* series) by David
Cumming (Wayland, 1997)

India (Cultural Journeys series) by Paul
Dash (Wayland, 1998)

Life Stories: Ghandi by Peggy Burns
(Wayland, 1993)

Stories from India by Vayu Naidu
(Wayland, 2000)

Films

Gandhi A dramatization of the life of
India's most famous leader.
Salaam Bombay A realistic portrayal of
street children in Bombay.
Heat and Dust Contrasting stories of a
woman living in 1920s colonial India
and her niece who arrives there
60 years later.

Index

Numbers in **bold** refer to illustrations.